The Little Book of Senior Moments

Shelley Klein

Michael O'Mara Books Limited

First published in Great Britain in 2008 by
Michael O'Mara Books Limited
9 Lion Yard
Tremadoc Road
London SW4 7NQ

A CIP catalogue record for this book is available from the British Library.

Papers used by Michael O'Mara Books Limited are natural, recyclable
products made from wood grown in sustainable forests. The manufacturing
processes conform to the environmental regulations of the country of
origin.

ISBN: 978-1-78243-140-4 in paperback print format

2 3 4 5 6 7 8 9 10

Designed and typeset by Design 23

Printed and bound by CPI Group (UK) Ltd, Croydon, CR0 4YY

www.mombooks.com

'I think the life cycle is all backwards. You should die first, get it out of the way. Then you live in an old-age home. You get kicked out when you're too young, you get a gold watch, you go to work. You work forty years until you're young enough to enjoy your retirement. You do drugs, alcohol, you party, you get ready for high school. You go to grade school, you become a kid, you play, you have no responsibilities, you become a little baby, you go back into the womb, you spend your last nine months floating . . . and you finish off as an orgasm.'

GEORGE CARLIN, COMEDIAN

INTRODUCTION

Senior moments are perhaps best described as the sort of mental blips that waylay us at the most inconvenient times; sometimes leading to confusion and calamity, they can be infuriating and entertaining in equal measure. Senior moments can strike even the best of us at an early age and the usual reaction to them is one of utter incredulity. However cruel it may seem, if the name of those oval-shaped objects you keep in the fridge which you can fry, boil or scramble for breakfast, is proving more difficult to conjure up than world peace, it may be time to face the music and embrace this new, brain-addled chapter of your life.

Overnight – or so it appears – you start

forgetting your own phone number. Then you mix your phone number up with your pin number, followed swiftly by attempting to use your pin number to access your credit card account. The day before yesterday you managed to mistake next door's house for your own and tried to unlock the front door, only to realize that instead of picking up the house keys on the way out you accidentally grabbed the keys to the garden shed. Don't go booking yourself in to a lunatic asylum, for all of the above are yet more examples of senior moments. Enjoy them, relish them, laugh at them, bask in them, but most of all – get used to having them, because from the moment they first rear their mischievous little heads, they will continue to plague you for the rest of your life.

The most important thing of all to remember is that when a senior moment does strike, do not feel foolish, annoyed or embarrassed, because it's certain that everyone, from the lowliest brain to the world's greatest thinkers, will have suffered the same.

EARLY SIGNS

Often, although we suspect we've begun experiencing senior moments, rather than recognizing the warning signs and acknowledging the facts, we bury our heads in the sand or, worse still, turn tail and run. Of course, these avoidance tactics are about as useful as a sledgehammer to the head. Here are some ways to detect whether you too are in the grip of this dreaded phenomenon:

You start calling your best friend of twenty-five years 'Thingy'.

You discover that your car has mysteriously parked itself on the other side of the road.

You could paint a picture of it, write a thesis about it, demonstrate how to use it to Olympic standard . . . but you can't for the life of you remember its name.

When you stand at the bottom of the stairs, you can't recall whether you were just about to go up to fetch something or whether you've just come down to fetch something.

You put all the photos you own into a large album, but, try as you might, you can't remember who any of the people are in the photographs.

You've started forgetting simple words such as . . . umm, uhhh, ahh . . .

The list of things you hate begins to outnumber the list of things you like.
You tend to go to restaurants that don't play music – this way you can enjoy hearing what everyone is saying.

You ring someone up but the moment they answer the phone you forget a) who you are calling, b) why you are calling, and c) why you are still living at all.

You start answering your phone . . . when it rings on television.

You start going through red traffic lights, but stopping at green ones.

You accidentally open your outgoing post . . . on a regular basis.

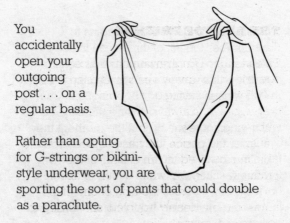

Rather than opting for G-strings or bikini-style underwear, you are sporting the sort of pants that could double as a parachute.

You are the last to admit that your 'get up and go' has got up and left.

THE BEST OF FRIENDS

Two well-bred Englishwomen of a certain age, friends for many years, met once a week in Oxford in order to go shopping; that done, they would then always reward themselves with tea at Fuller's.

On one occasion, they had settled at their table and ordered tea and slices of the famous walnut cake, when a look of absolute horror passed across the face of one of the ladies. Clearly deeply troubled, she turned to her companion and said:

'My dear, the most dreadful thing has happened. We have been friends for so many years, we see each other regularly and speak often, but suddenly and unaccountably, I have forgotten your name. I am sure that it will come to me in a moment, but could you possibly just tell me what it is? I really am most dreadfully sorry . . . '

Her friend stared at her in silence, frowning and obviously thinking very hard. The pause lengthened, as she gave all her attention to what her companion had just said. Finally, after the wait had lengthened to some minutes, she replied: 'When do you need to know by?'

HOW TIME FLIES

At an old soldiers' club, an old field marshal says to an equally old major general, 'Um, tell me, Charles, when did you last have sex with a woman?'

Charles scratches his head, ponders for a while and eventually answers: 'About 1946, I think, William. What about you, old chap?' William sighs and replies, 'That would be, um, 1948, I think.'

Charles shakes his head slowly and says, 'A long time ago, old boy, a long time ago.'

'Oh, I don't know,' says William, 'It's only just gone half past nine now, you know.'

MORE EARLY SIGNS

'Old age is like everything else. To make a success of it, you've got to start young.'
        FRED ASTAIRE, DANCER, SINGER AND ACTOR

'To me old age is fifteen years older than I am.'
        BERNARD M. BARUCH, FINANCIER AND STATESMAN

'There are three signs of old age: loss of memory . . . I forget the other two.'
        RED SKELTON, ACTOR

'Remembering something at first try is now as good as an orgasm as far as I'm concerned.'
        GLORIA STEINEM, FEMINIST AND JOURNALIST

'Spare a thought for my friend Eliza Hamilton, who was wrongly diagnosed as mentally unstable when all she was, was a bit giddy.'

MRS MERTON, *THE MRS MERTON SHOW*

'You remind me of a poem I can't remember, and a song that may never have existed, and a place I'm not sure I've ever been to.'

GRAMPA SIMPSON, *THE SIMPSONS*

'I've started wearing cardigans and saying things like "Whoopsadaisy", and when I take a first sip of tea, "Ooh, that hits the spot!"'

GARY, *MEN BEHAVING BADLY*

FAMILY REUNION

An elderly man in Australia calls his son in London and says, 'I hate to ruin your day, but I have to let you know that your mother and I have decided to separate – forty years of misery is enough for anybody.'

'Dad, I can't believe it!' his son exclaims.

'We can't stand the sight of each other, any longer,' the old man says. 'We're sick of each other, and I'm fed up of talking about it, so you call your sister in New York and tell her.' He hangs up the phone. Out of his mind with worry, the son calls his sister, who explodes down the phone.

'They simply cannot get a divorce,' she shouts. 'Leave it to me.' She calls her father immediately and screams at the old man, 'You are not divorcing mum! Please don't do a single thing until I get there. I'll call my brother now and we'll both be there tomorrow morning. Until then, don't do a thing, promise me?' and she hangs up. The old man puts down the receiver and turns to his wife.

'Okay,' he says, 'They're coming for Christmas and they're paying their own air fares.'

IT'S A NUMBERS THING

'I'm not interested in age. People who tell me their age are silly. You're as old as you feel.'

ELIZABETH ARDEN, BUSINESSWOMAN

'I can lie convincingly about my age because at my age I can't always remember what it is.'

VIOLET CONTI

'We're obsessed with age. Numbers are always and pointlessly attached to every name that's published in a newspaper: "Joe Creamer, forty-three, and his daughter, Tiffany-Ann, nine, were merrily chasing a bunny, two, when Tiffany-Ann tripped on the root of a tree, 106."'   JOAN RIVERS, COMEDIAN

'The years between fifty and seventy are the hardest. You are always being asked to do things, and you are not yet decrepit enough to turn them down.'

T. S. ELIOT, POET

'At twenty we worry about what others think of us; at forty we don't care about what others think of us; at sixty we discover they haven't been thinking about us at all.'

ANON

'I refuse to admit that I am more than fifty-two, even if that does make my sons illegitimate.'

NANCY ASTOR, SOCIALITE AND POLITICIAN

BACKSEAT DRIVER

An elderly lady dials the police to report that her car has been broken into. She is hysterical as she explains her situation.

'The monsters have stolen the stereo, the steering wheel, the brake pedal and even the accelerator!' she cries. The operator asks her to remain calm and informs her that a police officer is on his way. A few minutes later, the officer radios in his report.

'Disregard,' he says. 'She got in the backseat by mistake.'

KEEP DEATH OFF THE ROADS

A sixty-five-year-old man had just driven on to the motorway when his car phone rang. Answering it, he found his wife on the other end of the line.

'Bert,' she said urgently, 'Be careful. I've just heard on the news that there's a car driving the wrong way up the motorway.'

'Hell,' he replied. 'It's not just one – there are hundreds of them!'

GRUMPY OLD PEOPLE

Senior moments often go hand in hand with grumpy thoughts. Indeed, railing against the world is a sure sign that you are heading towards your dotage. Here are a few prime examples:

'Two elderly women are in a restaurant and one of 'em says, ''Boy, the food in this place is really terrible.'' The other one says, ''Yeah, I know, and such small portions.'' Well, that's essentially how I feel about life. Full of loneliness and misery and suffering . . . and it's all over much too soon.' WOODY ALLEN, DIRECTOR AND SCREENWRITER

'In my day, a juvenile delinquent was a kid who owed tuppence on an overdue library book.' MAX BYGRAVES, SINGER AND SONGWRITER

'At a certain age, you begin to snort at fashion, you stop going to the cinema and you watch the black-and-white classic on aeroplanes. You slouch into a curmudgeonly comfort culture of the old and familiar, and become a "call that" person. "Call that music/fashion/poetry/a chair?"'

A. A. GILL, NEWSPAPER COLUMNIST AND WRITER

'In my day, we never got woken up by a teasmade. We were knocked up every morning by a man with a six-foot pole. And we weren't having hysterectomies every two minutes either, like the girls these days. If something went wrong down below, you kept your gob shut and turned up the wireless.'

VICTORIA WOOD, *OLD BAG*

'In my day, men wore driving gloves, women stayed married, and curry had raisins in it.'

SWISS TONY, *THE FAST SHOW*

'If you are sufficiently irascible, God might just decide to wait.'

GODFREY JUST

'When you are about thirty-five years old, something terrible always happens to music.'

STEVE RACE, BROADCASTER, MUSICIAN AND AUTHOR

LOVE POTIONS

A man aged eighty-five and his eighty-year-old fiancée are over the moon about their decision to get married. One afternoon, they are taking a walk in order to discuss their

impending
nuptials when
they pass a
chemist and
Albert
suggests that
they go in.
Entering the
shop, he approaches the gentleman behind
the counter and asks whether he is the
owner. The pharmacist nods politely.

'Do you sell heart medication?' asks
Albert cheerfully.

'Of course we do, sir,' replies the
pharmacist and he reaches behind the
counter and produces the requested item.

'How about medicine for high blood
pressure?'

The pharmacist again nods and produces another package from behind the counter.

'Medicine for arthritis?'

'Yes, sir.'

'What about sleeping pills?'

'Yes, of course.'

'Vitamins?'

'Yes, a number of different types.'

'Oh, and do you stock Viagra?'

'Certainly.'

'That's great! We'd like to register here for our wedding gifts.'

WISE COUNSEL?

'[The late barrister] Patrick Pakenham became something of a legal legend . . . As defence counsel in a complicated fraud case, he was due to address the court during the afternoon session, and had partaken of a particularly well-oiled lunch. "Members of the jury, it is my duty to explain the facts in this case on my client's behalf; the judge will guide you and advise you on the correct interpretation of the law and you will then consider your verdict."

"Unfortunately," Pakenham went on, "for reasons which I won't go into now, my grasp of the facts is not as it might be. The judge is nearing senility; his knowledge of the law is pathetically out of date, and will be of no use in assisting you to reach a verdict. While, by the look of you, the possibility of your reaching a coherent verdict can be excluded." He was led from the court.'

THE DAILY TELEGRAPH

SMOKERS RULE

Actor George Burns, famed for his love of fine cigars, was a long-time member of the exclusive Hillcrest Country Club in Los Angeles. When Burns complained one day about the club's new ban on smoking, a sign was promptly posted for the comedian's benefit: 'Cigar smoking prohibited for anyone under ninety-five.'

A ROSE BY ANY OTHER NAME

Two elderly men, Ernest and Philip, are having lunch together, when Ernest turns to his friend and says, 'My wife and I went to a wonderful restaurant last night.'

'What was it called?' asks Philip, noticing the sudden look of confusion clouding his friend's face.

'What's the name of that flower that women like to get?' asks Ernest.

'A carnation?' suggests Philip.

'No.' Ernest frowns and looks thoughtful, before adding, 'It's red and has big petals.'

'Poppy?'

'No. It has a thorny stem.'

'Oh,' Philip nods, 'you mean a rose?'

'That's it.' Rising from his chair, Ernest wanders over to the staircase and shouts upstairs, 'ROSE! What's the name of that restaurant we went to last night?'

WHAT THE DOCTOR ORDERED?

A seventy-five-year-old man goes to the doctor to get a physical and a few days later the doctor sees him walking down the street with a stunning young lady on his arm and a huge smile on his face.

A couple more days pass and the old man

returns to the doctor's surgery. After he has again examined the elderly man, the doctor writes him out a prescription and says, 'You're really doing great, aren't you?' The patient replies,

'Just doing what you said, Doctor: "Get a hot mamma and be cheerful." That's what you told me and that's what I've done.'

'Actually I said, "You've got a heart murmur, and be careful." Now, while you're here, why don't we check your hearing . . . ?'

PRACTICAL IDEAS TO KEEP THE MIND IN SHAPE AND SENIOR MOMENTS AT BAY

Given that everyone is prone to suffering senior moments, it is incredibly fortunate that there are so many ways in which we can, if not eradicate the problem entirely, then at least keep it at bay. Below are a few simple ideas on how to keep those mental faculties in tip-top shape:

• Take up chess, bridge or other games in which one has to plan out moves in advance in order to win. Large jigsaw puzzles are also good memory boosters since they require you to remember the precise shape and colour of hundreds of individual pieces.

• Crosswords are an excellent form of mental gymnastics, provided that you can a) find where you last put down your glasses and b) find the newspaper. Studies have shown that people who do crossword puzzles four days per week had a 48 per cent lower risk of developing dementia than those who did no crosswords at all.

• Painting is yet another marvellous way to keep the mind active and the soul replenished. Young and old alike can partake in this activity, but the concentration required is especially helpful to those who are beginning to lose the ability to think clearly. Planning out your painting, choosing the type of paints you want to use, the required brushes for the effect you wish to create, your colour palette – all of these things exercise your mental faculties.

• Never, ever, under any circumstance, allow yourself to be photographed. An unflattering snapshot can set your self-esteem back several centuries.

• Try to avoid being herded into categories such as 'over-forties' or 'over-fifties'. It is never good for the ego to mix with large numbers of people the same age as you.

• Yoga is an excellent activity for anyone experiencing the first aches and pains of seniordom. This ancient art not only helps to maintain a supple body, it will also nurture both mind and spirit, aiding with relaxation and rejuvenation. A word of warning, however, for those of you who have never practised yoga before: make sure you attend a beginner's class rather than trying to teach yourself out of a book, as some of the poses can leave you in very awkward positions!

LOVE BITES

An elderly couple are lying in bed one night. Turning to her husband, the wife asks, 'Do you remember when we first started dating and you used to hold my hand?' Her husband leans over unenthusiastically and takes hold of his wife's hand before trying to get back to sleep.

A few moments later she says, 'Do you remember our first kiss? You used to kiss me all the time.' Mildly irritated, her husband reaches across, gives his wife a quick peck on the cheek and settles down to sleep.

Thirty seconds later his wife pipes up, 'Then you used to bite my neck.'

Angrily, her husband throws back the duvet, clambers out of bed and storms out of the room.

'Where are you going?' she calls after him.

'To get my teeth!'

AGE BEFORE BEAUTY

"Twenty-four years ago, madam, I was incredibly handsome. The remains of it are still visible through the rifts of time. I was so handsome that women became spellbound. In San Francisco, in rainy seasons, I was frequently mistaken for a cloudless day.'

MARK TWAIN, WRITER

'Keep looking at my eyes, dahling. My ass is like an accordian.' TALLULAH BANKHEAD, ACTRESS

'Alas, after a certain age every man is responsible for his face.'
ALBERT CAMUS, WRITER AND PHILOSOPHER

'I have the body of an eighteen-year-old. I keep it in the fridge.'
SPIKE MILLIGAN, COMEDIAN AND WRITER

'So much has been said and sung of beautiful young girls, why don't somebody wake up to the beauty of old women?'
HARRIET BEECHER STOWE, WRITER

'I said to my husband, "My boobs have gone, my stomach's gone – say something nice

about my legs." He said, "Blue goes with everything."'
JOAN RIVERS, COMEDIAN

'Cut off my head and I am thirteen.'
COCO CHANEL, COUTURIER

'I knew I was going bald when it was taking longer and longer to wash my face.'
HARRY HILL, COMEDIAN

'Women are not forgiven for ageing. Robert Redford's lines of distinction are my old-age wrinkles.'
JANE FONDA, ACTRESS

'Is there anything worn under the kilt? No, it's all in perfect working order.'

SPIKE MILLIGAN, COMEDIAN AND WRITER

'Talk about getting old. I was getting dressed and a peeping tom looked in the window, took a look and pulled down the shade.'

JOAN RIVERS, COMEDIAN

'I think your whole life shows in your face and you should be proud of that.'

LAUREN BACALL, ACTRESS

ON THE INDIGNITIES OF AGE

At some time after 1955, when Sir Winston Churchill was in his eighties and had ceded

the premiership to Eden, but remained a
Member of Parliament, the politician was sitting
in an armchair in the Members' Bar of the
House of Commons. He was alone. Three young
Tory MPs entered and, failing to see the old boy
slouched in his armchair, began to chatter
loudly. It soon became clear that the Member
for Epping was the subject of their talk.

'You know,' one remarked, 'it's very sad
about old Winston. He's getting awfully forgetful.'

'Shame, isn't it?' said another. 'He's really
very doddery now, I gather.'

'Not only that,' added the third, 'but I've
heard that he's going a bit – you know – gaga.'

'Yesh,' rumbled a deep voice from the
nearby armchair, 'an' they shay he'sh getting
terribly deaf, as well!'

SEEING RED

Two elderly women, Bessie and Eva, are out driving in a car and neither can see over the dashboard. Bessie is at the wheel and Eva is in the passenger seat. As they are cruising along, the car arrives at an intersection. The traffic light is red but Bessie drives straight through. Eva thinks to herself, 'I must be

losing it, I could have sworn we just went through a red light.'

After a few more minutes they come to another intersection. The light is again set to red and again they drive straight through. This time, Eva is almost sure that the light was red, but she is also concerned that she might be seeing things. Looking nervously over at her companion, she decides to pay very close attention at the next set of lights.

When the car approaches the next intersection the light is definitely red and Bessie drives straight through it for a third time. Turning to her friend, Eva says, 'Bessie! Do you know we just ran through three red lights in a row? You could have killed us.'

Eva turns to her companion and asks, 'Oh dear, am I driving?'

SENIOR SYMPHONY

One evening while attending one of George Gershwin's parties, Groucho Marx was approached by a fellow guest.

'Do you think Gershwin's melodies will be played a hundred years from now?' he asked.

'Sure,' Groucho replied, 'if George is here to play them.'

44

CATALOGUE OF COMPLAINTS

A group of senior citizens are discussing their various ailments in a nursing home one afternoon.

'I am so feeble that I can hardly lift this cup of coffee,' says one old lady.

'Tell me about it, my cataracts are so bad I can't even see what's on my plate,' replies another.

'I can't turn my head because of the arthritis in my neck.'

'My joints are so stiff and swollen that I have difficulty going to go to the bathroom at night.'

'Well, at least you're not incontinent, like me.'

'My blood-pressure pills make me dizzy,' another old lady continues, and several people nod in sympathetic agreement.

'I guess that's the price you pay for getting old,' sighs one old gentleman, slowly shaking his head.

'Well, it's not that bad,' said one woman cheerfully, 'at least we can still drive.'

SAY WHAT?

Two elderly women are eating breakfast one morning when one of them notices something funny about her friend's ear.

'Mildred, do you know you've got a suppository in your left ear?'

'Do I really? A suppository?' Mildred pulls it out and stares at it. 'Ethel, I'm glad you saw this thing. Now I know where my hearing aid is.'

TENDER MEMORY

A man walks into a bar and has a couple of beers. When he is finished the barman tells him that he owes £6.00.

'But I already paid, don't you remember?' asks the customer.

'Okay,' the barman agrees. 'If you say you paid, you paid.'

The man goes outside and tells the first person he sees that the barman can't keep track of whether his customers have paid or not. The second man then rushes in, orders a

47

beer and later tries the same trick. The bartender this time replies, 'If you say you paid, I'll take your word for it.'

The customer then goes into the street, sees an old friend and tells him how to get free drinks. The man hurries into the bar, orders three pints and begins to drink rapidly, when suddenly the bartender leans over and says, 'You know, a strange thing happened in here this afternoon. Two men were drinking beer, neither paid and both claimed that they did. The next person who tries that is going to regret it.'

'I'm sorry to hear that,' the final patron replies. 'Just give me my change and I'll be on my way.'

FREE-FALLING

During the filming of the 1998 thriller, *Crazy Six*, Burt Reynolds was determined to do his own stunts. 'Look, I can do this. I can still fall,' he told the film's producers. 'I just can't get up.'

REGRETS – I'VE HAD A FEW

'I rather regret I haven't taken more drugs. Is it too late, at seventy, to try cocaine? Would it be dangerous or interesting?'

JOAN BAKEWELL, JOURNALIST AND TV PRESENTER

'My one regret in life is that I am not someone else.'

WOODY ALLEN, DIRECTOR AND SCREENWRITER

'The only thing in my life that I regret is that I once saved David Frost from drowning. I had to pull him out, otherwise nobody would have believed I didn't push him in.'

PETER COOK, COMEDIAN

'If I had my life to live over, I'd live over a saloon.' W. C. FIELDS, COMEDIAN AND ACTOR

A DOUBLE LIFE

American comedian and entertainer Jack Benny often claimed to be thirty-nine years old. So it was fitting that Frank Sinatra's gift to Benny on his eightieth birthday was two copies of *Life Begins at 40*.

THREE LADIES

Three sisters aged sixty-five, seventy-five and seventy-seven years old all live together in the same house. The eldest sister goes upstairs to run a bath, puts her foot in the water, then shouts out, 'Was I getting out of this bath or getting in?'

The middle sister, who has been sitting downstairs reading a newspaper, gets up to help. She starts climbing the stairs, but then shouts out, 'Hey, am I coming down the stairs or going up them?'

The youngest sister, who has been drinking tea in the kitchen, lets out an enormous sigh and mutters under her breath, 'God, I hope I never get that forgetful,' knocking on wood for good measure.

'Okay,' she shouts out, 'I'll be up in a minute to help sort you out – I've just got to see who's at the door.'

IF YOU DON'T MOVE IT, YOU LOSE IT

'You gotta keep in shape. My grandmother started walking five miles a day when she was sixty. She's ninety-seven today and we don't know where the hell she is.'

ELLEN DEGENERES, ACTRESS AND COMEDIAN

'Health nuts are going to feel stupid someday, lying in hospitals dying of nothing.'

REDD FOXX, COMEDIAN

'To get back my youth, I would do anything in the world, except take exercise, get up early, or be respectable.'

OSCAR WILDE, PLAYWRIGHT AND NOVELIST

'Exercise is bunk. If you are healthy, you don't need it: if you are sick, you should not take it.'

HENRY FORD,
AUTOMOBILE
MANUFACTURER

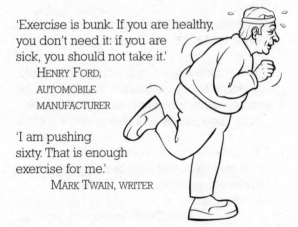

'I am pushing sixty. That is enough exercise for me.'

MARK TWAIN, WRITER

'I'm not feeling very well – I need a doctor immediately. Ring the nearest golf course.'
GROUCHO MARX, COMEDIAN AND ACTOR

'I exercise every morning without fail. Up, down! Up, down! And then the other eyelid.'
PHYLLIS DILLER, COMEDIAN

'I'd like to learn to ski, but I'm forty-four and I'm worried about my knees. They creak a lot and I'm afraid they might start an avalanche.'
JONATHAN ROSS, TV AND RADIO PRESENTER

'I now realize that the small hills you see on ski slopes are formed around the bodies of forty-seven-year-olds who tried to learn snowboarding.'
DAVE BARRY, WRITER AND COMEDIAN

ONE-TRACK MIND

On his eighty-ninth birthday, the French conductor Pierre Monteux was interviewed by the BBC. 'I still have two abiding passions,' he declared. 'One is my model railway, the other women. But at the age of eighty-nine, I find I am getting just a little too old . . . for model railways.'

OPEN-AND-SHUT CASE

When quizzed on how he retained his youthful appearance into his seventies, American entertainer Dick Clark replied, 'I keep an open mind . . . and a closed refrigerator.'

FOREVER YOUNG

'My recipe for perpetual youth? I've never had my face in the sun, and I have a very handsome young husband . . . Sex is one of the best and cheapest beauty treatments there is.'
                    JOAN COLLINS, ACTRESS AND WRITER

'Youth is a wonderful thing. What a crime to waste it on children.'
                    GEORGE BERNARD SHAW, WRITER

'My health is good; it's my age that's bad.'
                    RAY ACUFF, COUNTRY MUSIC SINGER

'I wish I was a twin, so I could know what I'd look like without plastic surgery.'

JOAN RIVERS, COMEDIAN

'I call them the lizard women. They're the ones who have had so much cosmetic surgery that they're no longer biodegradable. They look like giant Komodo dragons with Chanel accessories.'

BRETT BUTLER, COMEDIAN

'The secret of staying young is to live honestly, eat slowly, and lie about your age.'

LUCILLE BALL, ACTRESS

'Now I'm getting older I take health
supplements: geranium, dandelion,
passionflower, hibiscus. I feel great, and
when I pee, I experience the fresh scent of
pot pourri.'   SHEILA WENZ

'How foolish to think that one can ever slam
the door in the face of age. Much wiser to be
polite and gracious and ask him to lunch in
advance.' NOEL COWARD, ACTOR AND PLAYWRIGHT

'How does one keep from "growing old
inside"? Surely only in community. The only
way to make friends with time is to stay
friends with people . . . Taking community
seriously not only gives us the companionship
we need, it also relieves us of the notion that
we are indispensable.'   ROBERT MCAFEE BROWN

'Old Father Time will turn you into a hag if you don't show the bitch who's boss.'

MAE WEST, ACTRESS

'I don't plan to grow old gracefully. I plan to have facelifts until my ears meet.'

RITA RUDNER, COMEDIAN AND WRITER

HOLDING BACK THE YEARS

A lady goes into a cosmetics shop to buy a new anti-ageing face cream which, according to the advert, is 'guaranteed' to make the years drop off. Following the instructions carefully, she religiously applies just the right amount twice a day, and waits expectantly for the results.

After a few weeks, she decides that it's time to see if her husband has noticed any difference. One evening before bed she plucks up the courage to ask him.

'Darling, tell me the truth, what age would you say I am?'

Looking her up and down, her husband replies, 'Well, Susan, judging from your skin – twenty; your hair – eighteen; and your figure – twenty-five.'

'Oh, you flatterer!' she gushes, before kissing him.

'Hey, wait a minute,' he interrupts, 'I haven't added them up yet.'

RICH MAN

The aptly-named entertainer Harry Richman was occasionally known to tip a waiter fifty dollars simply after being handed the menu. Richman once asked a head waiter, 'What's the biggest tip you've ever received?'

'A hundred dollars,' the waiter replied. Richman gave the man two hundred dollars.

'Now tell me,' Richman asked, 'who gave you the hundred?'

'You did, Mr. Richman,' the waiter replied.

OVER THE HILL?

So there you are, skipping along life's uneven path, when suddenly a young whippersnapper comes along to trip you up by pointing out that you are not only over the hill, but tumbling down the other side. It is invariably those younger than yourself who seem to think they have a God-given right to point this fact out. Indeed, the cult of youth is almost single-handedly responsible for giving old age an image akin to that of the plague. In former centuries, those members of an older generation were regarded as sages and philosophers to look up to and respect. Nowadays, quite the opposite is true, with the general consensus being that if you aren't in your teens or early twenties, you might as well order your coffin now and be done with it. And, if you don't believe it, take a look at the following quotes:

'I can't wait until I'm thirty and I give up modelling because I'll be wrinkly and my bottom will be sagging . . . '

JODIE KIDD, *DAILY MAIL*

'The sight of an old woman [Joan Collins] still apparently believing that self-esteem depends on looking good and having a man is profoundly depressing, not to mention exhausting.'

FRANCES TAYLOR, *THE TIMES*

'Discussing the forthcoming contest to fill the gap that will be left on the *Today* programme when Sue McGregor steps down as a presenter, the editor Rod Liddle commented: "It would be nice to have a few people under forty with a bit of edge to them."'   *NEW STATESMAN*

'Here is proof that no one makes the case for natural boobs better than Madonna. At forty-four, she may be getting on a bit . . .'   *THE SUN*

'Two years ago I was at a lakeside trying to negotiate a speedboat ride for my daughter and two of my nieces. The man I was haggling with quoted an outrageous price. Taken by surprise, I said, "How much?"

   "What's the matter, Pops," he said, "losing your hearing also?"

"Pops? POPS! Do I look like a Pops?" I thought. "And what does he mean by 'also'?"

I bent over and, Narcissus style, looked at my reflection in the water. He was right. Peter Pan was nowhere to be seen. Sardonic middle age looked up at me from the water. You are getting old, Father William.'

ELIAKIM KATZ, WRITER

'Grey-haired men look "distinguished"? Surely the word is "extinguished".'

JULIE BURCHILL, JOURNALIST

'His toupee makes him look twenty years sillier.' BILL DANA, *NEW STATESMAN*

'While some of her fans will welcome another chance to see Cilla Black's shapely pins, others will be wondering whether a woman on the verge of her bus pass should be showing a little more decorum.' *DAILY MAIL*

'There aren't many actors of [Michael Caine's] vintage who are playing parts which suggest that the life force is still very much intact, without humiliating themselves by agreeing to be presented as romantic leads for actresses half their age.' *THE TIMES MAGAZINE*

'As a responsible grandfather, Tony Booth has given up drink and is now washed, pressed, trimmed and neat, like a pensioner on an outing.' JANE KELLY, *DAILY MAIL*

'I see Kirk Douglas still isn't dead.' JOHN PATTERSON, *THE GUARDIAN*

'He [Edward Fox] may be sixty-eight, but apart from the deep valleys and crevices in his stern, craggy face, there is no suggestion that he has "gone off".' SHOLTO BYRNES, JOURNALIST

'She [Catherine Zeta-Jones] looks like Sophia Loren on steroids. She's trussed up like a fifty-year-old, which is a shame because she's so beautiful, petite and delicate.'
SUSANNAH CONSTANTINE, TV PRESENTER

'The invite for *Top of the Pops* reads: "Over-18s but no wrinklies". Most of the audience weren't even born the last time David Cassidy was famous. Any older fans that do get into the studio will have their grey heads edited out of the broadcast.'
NICK CURTIS, *EVENING STANDARD*

'*Sex and the City* star Kim Cattrall has complained that she is finding it hard to get a date. Well, dear, it's what you should expect at forty-six. As we get older we all begin to have difficulty with dates, names, where we parked . . .'   THE SUNDAY TIMES

'Elle Macpherson has just come back from two months in Ibiza . . . the break seems to have paid off because, even at thirty-seven, Elle looks very, very lovely.'

SIMON MILLS, EVENING STANDARD

'Greta Scacchi, at forty-one, still has the looks of a Hollywood star.'

RYAN GILBEY, THE INDEPENDENT

TILL MEMORY LOSS DO US PART

Doris Day was walking down the street in Beverly Hills one day when she was stopped by a man. Assuming that he was a fan, Day said hello and continued on her way. 'Don't you remember me?' the man called after her.

'No,' the actress replied. 'Should I?' 'Well, you didn't have that many husbands,' replied her second husband, saxophonist George Weidler.

THE TIME OF YOUR LIFE

'Write, paint, sculpt, learn the piano, take up dancing, whether it's the tango or line dancing, start a college course, fall in love all over again – the possibilities are limitless for you to achieve your private ambitions.'

JOAN COLLINS, ACTRESS AND WRITER

'You're never too old. A person of sixty can grow as much as a child of six. Michelangelo did some of his best paintings when past eighty; George Bernard Shaw was still writing plays at ninety; Grandma Moses didn't even begin painting until she was seventy-nine.'

MAXWELL MALTZ, COSMETIC SURGEON AND WRITER

'When you're young, you don't know, but you don't know you don't know, so you take some chances. In your twenties and thirties, you don't know, and you know you don't know, and that tends to freeze you; less risk taking. In your forties you know, but you don't know you know, so you may still be a little tentative. But then, as you pass fifty, if you've been paying attention, you know, and you know you know. Time for some fun.'

GEORGE CARLIN, COMEDIAN

'Develop interest in life as you see it: in people, things, literature, music – the world is so rich, simply throbbing with treasures, beautiful souls and interesting people. Forget yourself.'   HENRY MILLER, WRITER

'I am more alive than most people. I am an electric eel in a pond of goldfish.'

EDITH SITWELL, POET AND CRITIC

BODY SNATCHER

Senior moments aren't just confined to having problems remembering things – often a senior moment is experienced when you realize your body is not quite what it once was: 'I don't actually inhabit my body any more. At some point somebody came along, body snatched, gave me this. It's the kind of body I used to look at on beaches and think, "Goodness me, how does that happen? How could you let yourself go like that?" That's how it happens – it just happens.'

KATHRYN FLETT, WRITER

FORGET ME NOT

An eighty-five-year-old man marries a beautiful twenty-two-year-old woman. Because her husband is so old, his bride decides that on their wedding night they should sleep in separate beds. The last thing she wants is for him to overexert himself on their first night together as man and wife.

After the wedding the young lady gets ready for bed, climbs under the covers and waits expectantly. Sure enough, she hears a knock. The door opens, and there stands her husband, ready for action. When they have finished making love, the old man leaves and his young wife prepares to sleep.

A few minutes pass before the woman is awoken by another knock on her bedroom door. Surprised to find her husband there again, she lets him in and is astonished by his sexual prowess. When they are finished, the old man kisses his wife, bids her goodnight and leaves.

Exhausted by this time, the young woman is ready to go to sleep again. However, after a space of just a few minutes, there follows another knock at her door and there stands the groom again, as fresh as a twenty-five-year-old and ready for a bit more action.

When he is once again set to leave, his bride turns to him and says, 'I'm amazed, sweetheart. I've been with men a quarter of your age who were good only once! You're a fantastic lover.'

Somewhat embarrassed, the old man scratches his head, turns to his wife and says, 'You mean I've been here already?'

IDENTITY CRISIS

One of the many funny stories told about President George Bush concerns a visit he made to an old people's home. After speaking to a few of the residents, The President asked of one old lady, 'Do you know who I am?'

'No,' came the snappy reply, 'but I'm sure if you ask at reception they'll be able to tell you.'

PRAISE INDEED

Producer Samuel Goldwyn was filming one day when someone on set is said to have told him that one of his productions was magnificent.

'Magnificent,' Goldwyn was said to have snapped. 'It's more than magnificent – it's MEDIOCRE!'

GOLDEN OLDIES – SECRETS OF LONGEVITY

'Scientists say that women who have children after forty are more likely to live to be 100, but they don't know why. I think the reason is, they're waiting for the day when their kids move out of the house.'   LORRIE MOSS

'To what do I attribute my longevity? Bad luck, mostly.'

BILLY WILDER, SCREENWRITER AND PRODUCER

'*Q.* What is the secret of your long life?
A. Keep breathing.'

SOPHIE TUCKER, SINGER AND COMEDIAN

'Alcohol is good for you. My grandfather proved it irrevocably. He drank two quarts of booze every mature day of his life and lived to the age of 103. I was at the cremation – the fire would not go out.'

DAVE ASTOR, NEWSPAPER PUBLISHER

'Age is an issue of mind over matter. If you don't mind, it doesn't matter.'

MARK TWAIN, WRITER

'At seventy, I'm in fine fettle for my age, sleep like a babe and feel around twelve. The secret? Lots of meat and cigarettes and not giving in to things.'
JENNIFER PATTERSON, JOURNALIST AND TV PRESENTER

LONG DIVISION

Upon the occasion of his turning eighty, American vaudeville singer Sophie Tucker's ex-husband informed her of a new development in his love life. The octogenarian allegedly rang up his former wife and said, 'Soph! Soph! I just married myself a twenty-year-old girl. What do you think of that?'

Tucker's response swiftly followed. 'Ernie, when I am eighty I shall marry me a twenty-year-old boy. And let me tell you something,

Ernie: twenty goes into eighty a helluva lot more than eighty goes into twenty!'

LIFE IS . . .

'Life is a moderately good play with a badly written third act.'   TRUMAN CAPOTE, WRITER

'Life is a funny thing that happens to you on the way to the grave.'
                    QUENTIN CRISP, WRITER AND ACTOR

'Life is available to anyone no matter what age. All you have to do is grab it.'
                              ART CARNEY, ACTOR

'Life is a marathon in which you reserve the

sprint for the end. Mentally I pace myself. I have got an energy bank account and I can't afford to be overdrawn.'

PETER USTINOV, WRITER AND ACTOR

'Life can only be understood backwards, but it must be lived forwards.'

SØREN KIERKEGAARD, PHILOSOPHER

'Life is rather like opening a tin of sardines. We're all of us looking for the key.'

ALAN BENNETT, WRITER AND ACTOR

'Life is too short, but it would be absolutely awful if it were too long.'

PETER USTINOV, WRITER AND ACTOR

LATE BLOOMERS

You are never too old to
achieve your goals.
Experience is a fine thing
and it is never too late to
see the world in new
and different ways.
Just take a look at the
following senior success
stories for inspiration:

• George Burns won his first
Oscar at the age of eighty.

• The author Mary Wesley, who wrote *The
Camomile Lawn*, had her first novel published
after the age of seventy.

• Painter Grandma Moses painted her first picture when she was past eighty years old, completing over 1,500 paintings during the rest of her life.

• Michelangelo was seventy-one when he painted the ceiling of the Sistine Chapel.

• Physician and humanitarian Albert Schweitzer was still performing operations in his African hospital at the age of eighty-nine.

• Marc Chagall, aged ninety, became the first living artist to be exhibited at the Louvre.

• Pablo Picasso produced drawings and engravings into his nineties.

• Italian sculptor, architect and painter Gian Lorenzo Bernini began designing churches aged sixty.

• Physicist William Sturgeon created the first electromagnet at the age of forty.

• Herman Hesse wrote *Steppenwolf* at the age of fifty.

OLD AGE IS . . .

'Old age is remembering Cup Final teams and goals of generations past far more vividly than you can those of, well, only two days ago.'   FRANK KEATING, POLITICIAN

'By the time we've made it, we've had it.'
MALCOLM FORBES, PUBLISHER OF *FORBES* MAGAZINE

'Old age equalizes – we are aware that what is happening to us has happened to untold numbers from the beginning of time. When we are young, we act as if we were the first young people in the world.' ERIC HOFFER, WRITER

SILVER LININGS

'One pleasure attached to growing older is that many things seem to be growing younger; growing fresher and more lively than we once supposed them to be.'
G. K. CHESTERTON, WRITER

'*Q.* You're eighty-six years old. You smoke ten cigars a day, drink five martinis a day, surround yourself with beautiful women. What does your doctor say about all this? *A.* My doctor is dead.'

GEORGE BURNS, ACTOR AND WRITER

'How pleasant is the day when we give up striving to be young – or slender.'
WILLIAM JAMES, PSYCHOLOGIST AND PHILOSOPHER

'I always make a point of starting the day at 6 a.m. with champagne. It goes straight to the heart and cheers one up. White wine won't do. You need the bubbles.'
JOHN MORTIMER, WRITER AND DRAMATIST

'Wrinkles should merely indicate where smiles have been.' MARK TWAIN, WRITER

'The spiritual eyesight improves as the physical eyesight declines.' PLATO, PHILOSOPHER

'Give me chastity and continence, but not yet.'
SAINT AUGUSTINE

'The great thing about getting older is that you don't lose all the other ages you've been.'
MADELEINE L'ENGLE, WRITER

'There is more felicity on the far side of baldness than young men can possibly imagine.'
LOGAN PEARSALL SMITH, WRITER

'Now I'm getting older, I don't need to do drugs any more. I can get the same effect just by standing up real fast.'
JONATHAN KATZ, COMEDIAN AND ACTOR

'No pleasure is worth giving up for the sake of two more years in a geriatric home in Weston-super-Mare.'
KINGSLEY AMIS, WRITER

'These are the soul's changes. I don't believe in ageing. I believe in forever altering one's aspect to the sun. Hence my optimism.'

VIRGINIA WOOLF, WRITER

'The joy of being older is that in one's life one can, towards the end of the run, overact appallingly.'

QUENTIN CRISP, WRITER AND ACTOR

'Sometimes it's fun to sit in your garden and try to remember your dog's name.'

STEVE MARTIN, ACTOR AND COMEDIAN

'One of the advantages of being seventy is that you need only four hours' sleep. True, you need it four times a day, but still.'
    DENIS NORDEN, COMEDIAN AND TV PRESENTER

'As you grow old, you lose your interest in sex, your friends drift away, your children often ignore you. There are many other advantages, of course, but these would seem to be the outstanding ones.'
    RICHARD NEEDHAM, *TORONTO GLOBE AND MAIL*

'If I'm feeling really wild, I don't bother flossing before bedtime.'
                    JUDITH VIORST, PRESENTER

'The nice thing about being old is that it doesn't affect your betting; in fact, old people betting makes more sense than young people betting. The lady in the bookies said to me, "Do you like having a little bet?" I told her no, I loathed it. I like to make big bets.'
CLEMENT FREUD, WRITER AND BROADCASTER

OLD GIRLS' REUNION

When a studio usher knocked on the door of Ethel Barrymore's Hollywood dressing room and announced that there were a couple of girls hanging about outside who said they went to school with her, and enquired as to what he should do, Barrymore's reply came quickly: 'Wheel them in.'

TIME'S WINGED CHARIOT

'Most of us spend our lives as if we had
another one in the bank.'   BEN IRWIN

'As I get older the years just fly by. I don't
think there was an April this year.'
                              JEREMY HARDY, COMEDIAN

'Half our life is spent trying to find something
to do with the time we have rushed through
life trying to save.'
          WILL ROGERS, COMEDIAN AND ENTERTAINER

'One day, aged forty-five, I just went into the
kitchen to make myself a cup of tea, and
when I came out I found I was sixty-eight.'
                              THORA HIRD, ACTRESS

EARLY TO BED

Two teenage girls (yes, senior moments can strike at any time) were taking a bus together when one was overheard saying to the other: 'The thing is I can't bear late nights. If I go out to dinner with friends and I'm not in bed by 11, I go home.'

THE PRIME OF LIFE?

One day in his eighty-seventh year, Justice Oliver Wendell Holmes Jr. is rumoured to have passed a beautiful girl while out walking with an old friend.

'Oh,' he sighed, turning to watch her as she walked away, 'to be seventy again!'

WEATHER OR NOT

Three retired gentlemen, each with bad hearing, are playing golf on a blustery afternoon. One remarks to the other, 'Windy, isn't it?'

'No,' the second man replies, 'it's Thursday.' And the third man chimes in, 'So am I. There's a pub just round the corner.'

ONE FOR THE ROAD

One day while out patrolling the motorway for speeding drivers, a policeman stopped a car that had been doing ninety-miles an hour. The driver, none too impressed at being stopped by the long arm of the law, began being quite rude to the officer.

His wife, who was in the passenger seat, thinking she would try and come to her husband's rescue, leant over him and in a blind senior panic said as sweetly as possible, 'Please don't take too much notice of him officer, he's always like this after he's had a few down the pub.'

AGE DEFIES GRAVITY

One evening late in his life, former senator Chauncey Depew found himself seated at a dinner party beside a young woman in a low-cut, off-the-shoulder dress. Looking the scantily clad woman over, the senator leaned in towards her.

'My dear,' he asked, 'what is keeping that

dress on you?'
The woman's reply?
'Only your age, Mr Depew!'

THANKS FOR THE MEMORIES

On his way home from
work a young man
sees an old lady sitting
on a park bench,
crying her eyes out.
Stopping in concern,
he asks her what is
wrong.

'I have a fit young
husband who makes
love to me every

morning and then gets up and makes me pancakes with blueberries, sausages, bacon, fried eggs, mushrooms, fresh fruit and freshly ground coffee.'

'Well, why on earth are you crying, then?'

'Every day he makes me a delicious lunch of lamb chops and new potatoes, followed by chocolate cake, then we watch a film together and make love for the rest of the day.'

'Well, then why are you crying?'

'For dinner he makes me a gourmet meal with a bottle of red wine, and then we make love until two in the morning.'

Beginning to lose patience, the young man asks again, 'Why are you crying?' Shaking uncontrollably, the old woman sobs,

'I can't remember where I live!'

SHAKES-PEERING

When the poet W. H. Auden arrived to deliver
a lecture on Shakespeare at the New School
for Social Research in New York, he discovered
that every seat in the room had been filled.

'If there are any of you who do not hear me,'
Auden began, looking at the sea of faces in the
audience, 'please don't raise your hands,
because I am also near sighted.'

THE FOUR SEASONS

'The course of life is fixed, and nature admits of
its being run but in one way, and only once;
and to each part of our life there is something
seasonable; so that the feebleness of children,

as well as the high spirit of youth, the soberness of maturer years, and the ripe wisdom of old age – all have a certain natural advantage which would be secured in its proper season.'   CICERO, ON OLD AGE

TYPOS – FROM BAD TO WORSE

Typos are easily made and nowhere is this more apparent than in the newspaper industry. Having said that however, the typesetter at the New York American must have been suffering a bad case of senioritis when he printed 'battle-scared hero' instead of 'battle-scarred hero'. As if this wasn't embarrassing enough however, in later editions the mistake was corrected to read, 'bottle-scarred hero.'

BACK TO FRONT

The American Broadcaster and actor Harry
Von Zell was once asked to introduce the then
president of the United States, Herbert
Hoover. But while suffering what can only be
described as a rather unfortunate senior
moment he introduced his radio guest by
saying, 'Ladies and Gentlemen – the president
of the United States, Hoobert Herver!'

LIKE MOTHER, LIKE DAUGHTER!

While interviewing Liza Minelli (star of *Cabaret*)
on BBC TV *Nationwide*, the broadcaster Hugh
Scully suddenly became muddled and instead
of thanking his guest said, 'Thank you, Judy

Garland.' Ever quick off the mark, Minelli rallied round and replied, 'I'll tell Liza.'

THE PERKS OF SENIOR MOMENTITUS

It is reassuring to know that something as troublesome as senior momentitus can have a few perks . . .

• You can throw yourself a surprise party – just invite everyone you know, then forget all about it.

• You can buy your own Christmas presents, wrap them and not have a clue what they are when you come to open them.

• You can bake your own birthday cake and still imagine someone else has done it for you.

BABY, BABY

A fifty-one-year-old woman went to Italy to see a doctor who could help elderly women have babies. She soon fell pregnant and gave birth to a beautiful boy. All her friends and acquaintances loved the child, but one day one of her closest friends had to move away, so she decided to make one last visit to see her friend's child. The woman told her friend that the child was asleep, but that he would wake up soon and then she could cuddle him. However, as the hours passed by, the friend grew increasingly impatient. Finally, the new mother owned up.

'I have to wait for him to wake up and cry because I can't remember where I put him down to sleep!' she confessed sheepishly.

BRIDAL WHERE

Two men, one young and one old, are pushing trolleys around a supermarket when they bump into one another. The old guy says to the young guy, 'Sorry about that. I'm looking for my wife, and I guess I wasn't paying attention to where I was going.' The young man says, 'That's OK. What a coincidence! I'm looking for my wife, too. I can't find her anywhere and I'm getting desperate.' The old man replies, 'Well, maybe we can help each other. What does your wife look like?' The young man says, 'Well, she is twenty-six years old, with blonde hair, blue eyes, slim, busty and she's wearing a tight black mini-skirt. What does your wife look like?' The old man says, 'Doesn't matter, son . . . let's look for yours first.'

STANDING TO ATTENTION

A very elderly and frail gentleman turned to his equally old friend, Ernest, and asked if he could remember the name of the stuff the army used to put in their cups of tea during World War One, to stop the soldiers getting randy in the trenches. His companion remembered the ingredient, but was unable to recall its name. He asked, however, why his friend wanted to know. The answer was, 'Well, you know, Ernie, I think it's finally started to work.'

MISTAKEN IDENTITY

One evening, P. G. Wodehouse was sitting next to an elderly woman at dinner when she began lavishly praising him for his books. Apparently, her sons were huge fans of his work; they always bought his latest novels and their rooms were lined with his books. 'And when I tell them,' she concluded, 'that I have actually been sitting at dinner with Edgar Wallace, I don't know what they will say.'

TWICE AS FORGETFUL

An elderly couple were going away on holiday and stopped at a restaurant for lunch. After the meal, the elderly woman left her glasses on the table, but she didn't notice they were missing until they were back on the road. By this time, the old couple had to travel quite a distance before they could turn around.

The elderly man complained all the way back to the restaurant and muttered under his breath, calling his wife every terrible name he could think of. When the pair finally arrived at the

restaurant, and the old woman got out of the car to retrieve her glasses, her husband shouted after her, 'And while you're in there, you might as well get my teeth, too.'

ON THE MENU

A ninety-year-old man checked into a posh hotel to celebrate his birthday. As a surprise, a few of his friends sent a call girl to his room. When the man opened the door, he saw before him a beautiful young woman.

She said, 'I've brought you a present.'

He said, 'What is it?'

She said, 'I am yours for super sex.'

The old man replied, 'I'm ninety years old, I'll have the soup.'

THE NAME GAME

We all try our best to avoid senior moments. Some of us write lists or notes on the backs of our hands so as not to forget something important, while others ensure that they have at least sixteen sets of house keys hidden strategically around their property, so that they never find themselves locked out. However, for sheer gall, nothing quite beats the audacity or cunning of the man who admitted that he called all his girlfriends (at the time he had four) by the same nickname. This meant that he never made the mistake of waking up with one and calling her the wrong name. How's that for prevention being better than a cure?

A HELPFUL HUSBAND

Seventy-year-old Mrs Jones went to the doctor for her annual check-up. He told her that she needed more activity and recommended sex three times a week. She said to the doctor, 'Please, tell my husband.' The doctor went out to the waiting room and told Mr Jones that his wife needed to have sex three times a week. Her eighty-year-old husband replied, 'Which days?'

'How about Monday, Wednesday and Friday?'

'I can bring her in on Monday and Wednesday,' the man said, 'but on Friday she'll have to take the bus.'

MISSPELLED YOUTH

When the British poet and journalist J. C. Squire wrote an article about *A Midsummer Night's Dream*, he was somewhat amused to discover that the typesetter, in a moment of senioritis, had misspelled the name 'Hermia' and written 'Hernia' instead. Squire opted to leave the misspelling as it was, saying: 'I cannot bring myself to interfere with my printer's first fine careless rupture.'

MIAOW!

Every Sunday, a sweet little old lady went to her local church and placed £200 in the collection box. This carried on for months until one day the priest approached his parishioner and said, 'Excuse me, I couldn't help but notice that every Sunday you put £200 in our collection box.'

'Oh yes,' the little old lady replied blithely, 'my son lives over in America and sends me an awful lot of money every week, so what I don't need for myself, I give to the church.'

'But how much does he send you?' said the priest. 'Because £200 is an awful lot of money.'

'He gives me £1,000 per week,' she replied proudly.

'Your son must be very successful then. What does he do?'

'He's a vet.'

'What a good profession,' sighed the priest. 'Where is it he practises?'

'Oh well, he has one cat house in Kansas and the other in Vegas,' she replied.

TOILET TRAINING

Seventy-year-old John went for his annual physical. All of his tests came back with normal results. Dr Adams said, 'John, everything looks great physically. How are you doing mentally and spiritually? Are you at peace with yourself, and do you have a good relationship with God?'

John replied, 'God and I are close. He knows I have poor eyesight, so he has arranged that when I get up in the middle of the night to go to the bathroom the light goes on and when I've finished the light goes off.'

'Wow!' exclaimed Dr Adams. 'That's incredible!'

A little later in the day, Dr Adams called John's wife.

'Sarah,' he said, 'John is doing fine. Physically, he's great. But I had to call because I'm amazed by his relationship with God. Is it true that he gets up during the night and the light goes on in the bathroom and then when he is finished the light goes off?'

Sarah exclaimed, 'Oh my God! He's peeing in the refrigerator again!'

LANGUAGE BARRIER

A bilingual man went off to work in France. His elderly mother was anxious as she was used to speaking to him every day, but he reassured her that she could phone as often as she wanted.

Time passed after he'd arrived, however, and she didn't call once. Was it the cost? Had she lost the number? Concerned, he rang to find out.

'I tried to call you four times!' she said

angrily. 'Each time, a rude Frenchman spoke over the top of me. He made no attempt to listen to me or to fetch you. I don't want to talk to him again.'

The penny dropped. The old lady had been speaking to his answerphone message.

BLISSFUL SLUMBERS

'Oh, Sleep! it is a gentle thing
Beloved from pole to pole!'

SAMUEL TAYLOR COLERIDGE,
'THE RIME OF THE ANCIENT MARINER'

There can be no more pleasurable way to keep senior moments at bay and to maintain a youthful appearance than indulging in plenty of sleep. Indeed, it is essential that we enjoy plenty of sleep throughout our lives, but never is it more valuable than during our senior years.

If you find dropping off to sleep difficult, then perhaps you should revert to those tried-and-tested methods of a hot bath and a milky drink before bed. Reading will also help to relax the mind and prepare it for sleep. Other tips include:

- keeping your bedroom well aired

- drinking camomile tea before you go to bed

- counting sheep

SICK HUMOUR

Mrs Green called her doctor's surgery to find out her husband's test results.

'I'm so sorry,' the nurse told her, 'but there's been some sort of mistake. When we sent your husband's samples to the laboratory, some samples from another Mr Green were sent as well. One Mr Green has tested positive for Alzheimer's disease and the other Mr Green for syphilis. We can't tell which results are your husband's.'

'That's terrible,' cried Mrs Green. 'Can we do the test over again to find the answer?'

'Your Health Maintenance Organization won't pay for these expensive tests to be run twice.'

'Well, what are we supposed to do?'

THE LITTLE BOOK OF SENIOR MOMENTS

'The doctor recommends that you drop your husband off in the middle of town. If he finds his way home, don't sleep with him.'

POPPING THE QUESTION

An elderly man asked his wife of fifty years, 'If you had to do it over again, would you marry me?'

'You've asked me that before,' she answered.

'What did you reply?'

'I don't remember.'

HOW QUICKLY WE FORGET

Two elderly gentlemen, Roger and Ted, are sitting in rocking chairs outside their nursing home when a nice young woman walks past wearing a pink miniskirt.

Roger said, 'Ted, did you see that?'

Ted replied, 'Yes I did Roger, lovely wasn't she.'

Roger rocked a little faster in his chair, 'I'd like to take her out, wine her, dine her and . . . and . . . Ted what was that other thing we used to do?'

ON THE COUCH

A forgetful man goes to see a psychiatrist.

'My trouble is,' he says, 'that I keep forgetting things.'

'How long has this been going on?' asks the psychiatrist.

'How long has what been going on?' says the man.

SPENDING HABIT

While in the White House, John F. Kennedy found a note with the reminder 'Department store – $40,000'. Immediately recognizing his wife's handwriting, and familiar with Jackie's spendthrift habits, he confronted his wife.

'What the hell is this?' he quizzed her. Jackie glanced down at the note, considered for a moment, and said, 'I don't remember.'

LAST-MINUTE OBSERVATIONS PLUS A FEW EXTRA TIPS

'Anyone who stops learning is old, whether at twenty or eighty. Anyone who keeps learning stays young. The greatest thing in life is to keep your mind young.'

HENRY FORD, AUTOMOBILE MANUFACTURER

'Dying is no big deal. The least of us will manage that. Living is the trick. My life has been strawberries in the wintertime, and you can't ask for more than that.'   RED SMITH

'If I'm ever stuck on a respirator or a life-support system, I definitely want to be unplugged. But not until I'm down to a size 8.'

HENRIETTE MANTEL, ACTRESS

'We learn from experience that man never learns from experience.'

GEORGE BERNARD SHAW, PLAYWRIGHT

'Memorial services are the cocktail parties of the geriatric set.' JOHN GIELGUD, ACTOR

'Experience is a comb life gives you after you lose your hair.' JUDITH STERN

'Inside every seventy-year-old is a thirty-five-year-old asking, "What happened?"'

ANN LANDERS, ADVICE COLUMNIST

'I don't mind dying. Trouble is, you feel so bloody stiff the next day.'

GEORGE AXELROD, WRITER AND PRODUCER

'No matter how rich you become, how famous or powerful, when you die the size of your funeral will still pretty much depend on the weather.'

MICHAEL PRITCHARD, MOTIVATIONAL SPEAKER

'I expect you know the story of Winston [Churchill] in later years in the House of Commons. When a colleague tactfully told him that several of his fly buttons were undone, he said, "No matter. The dead bird does not leave the nest."'

RUPERT HART-DAVIS,
THE LYTTELTON – HART-DAVIS LETTERS

'Always have old memories and young hopes.' ARSENE HOUSSAYE, WRITER AND POET

'My dream is to die in a tub of ice cream, with Mel Gibson.'

JOAN RIVERS, COMEDIAN

'I am ready to meet my Maker. Whether my Maker is ready for the ordeal of meeting me is another matter.'

WINSTON CHURCHILL, FORMER PRIME MINISTER

'If logic tells you that life is a meaningless accident, don't give up on life. Give up on logic.'

SHIRA MILGROM

'One's first step to wisdom is to question everything – and one's last is to come to terms with everything.'

GEORG CHRISTOPH LICHTENBERG, PHYSICIST AND ASTRONOMER

'There's nothing like a morning funeral for sharpening the appetite for lunch.'

ARTHUR MARSHALL, WRITER AND BROADCASTER

'It was Death – possibly the only dinner guest more unwelcome than Sidney Poitier.'

KINKY FRIEDMAN, SINGER AND SONGWRITER

BIBLIOGRAPHY

Burningham, John. (Ed.)
The Time of Your Life – Getting On With Getting On
(BLOOMSBURY, 2002)

Chancellor, Alexander.
'Senior Disservice'
(*THE GUARDIAN*, 15 MAY 1999)

Clark, Alan.
Alan Clark: Diaries
(WEIDENFELD & NICHOLSON, 1993)

Corcoran, Alan, and Green, Joey.
Senior Moments
(SIMON & SCHUSTER, 2002)

Coward, Noel.
The Noel Coward Diaries
Edited by Graham Payn and Sheridan Morley
(WEIDENFELD & NICOLSON, 1982)

Enright, D. J.
Play Resumed – A Journal
(OXFORD UNIVERSITY PRESS, 1999)

Jarski, Rosemarie.
Wrinklies' Wit & Wisdom
(PRION, CARLTON PUBLISHING GROUP, 2005)

Mortimer, John.
The Summer of a Dormouse
(VIKING, 2000)

Priestley, J. B.
Outcries and Asides
(HEINEMANN, 1974)

Zobel, Allia.
The Joy of Being 50-Plus
(WORKMAN PUBLISHING, 1999)